Absence is the gauze of loss.

~ Candice James

Never part without loving words to think of during your absence.
It may be that you will not meet again in this life.

~ Jean Paul

In Absentia

Absence is the greatest loss.

— Caroline James

Not a day without loving words to think of during your absence.
Happy be that you will not moan again in this life.

— Lan (Fan)

IN ABSENTIA

BY

FABRICE POUSSIN

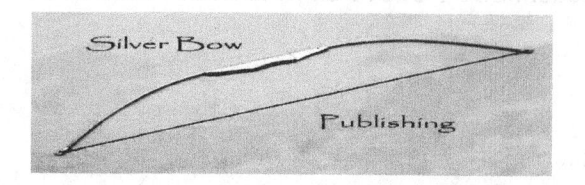

720 Sixth Street, Unit #5,
New Westminster, BC Canada
V3L 3C5

Title: In Absentia
Authors: Fabrice Poussin
Publisher: Silver Bow Publishing
Cover Photo: by Fabrice Poussin
Cover Design: Candice James
Layout and editing: Candice James

All rights reserved including the right to reproduce or translate this book or any portions thereof, in any form without the permission of the publisher. Except for the use of short passages for review purposes, no part of this book may be reproduced, in part or in whole, or transmitted in any form or by any means, electronically or mechanically, including photocopying, recording, or any information or storage retrieval system without prior permission in writing from the publisher or a license from the Canadian Copyright Collective Agency (Access Copyright). Copyright to all individual poems remains with the author.
© Silver Bow Publishing 2021

9781774031711 Print
9781774031728 epub

Library and Archives Canada Cataloguing in Publication

Title: In absentia / by Fabrice Poussin.
Names: Poussin, Fabrice, author.
Description: Poems.
Identifiers: Canadiana (print) 20210250364 | Canadiana (ebook) 20210250437 | ISBN 9781774031711
   (softcover) | ISBN 9781774031728 (Kindle)
Classification: LCC PS3616.O875 I5 2021 | DDC 811/.6—dc23

In Absentia

To my mom and dad
who are looking at each other as if saying,
"What has our son gotten himself into this time?"

To my friend and colleague, Angie O'Neal,
who encouraged me by simply saying, "You should do it!"

In Absentia

Contents

A Pile of Bones ... 11
Balancing into Life ... 12
Breaking Away ... 13
Brown Bags ... 14
Calling in Silence ... 15
Chest of Riches ... 16
Child Yet ... 17
Christmas in Barbed Wire ... 18
Collapse ... 19
Crannied Heart ... 20
Dreams of the Dying ... 21
Elegance ... 22
Eternity in a Vise ... 2
Exorcised ... 24
Explorer ... 25
Farewell ... 26
Fashioning a Friend ... 27
Fashioning Eternity ... 28
Fear of the Light ... 29
Feeding the Monsters ... 30
Final Talk ... 31
Fingerprints on Another Light ... 32
First Day ... 33
Flight of the Swallows ... 34
Floating ... 35
Free ... 36
Frozen Features ... 37
Gambling with My World ...38
Grace Undercover ... 39
Grounded ... 40
His Kingdom for a Touch ... 41
In Absentia ... 42
In Dali's World ... 43
In the Valley of the Gods ... 44

In Absentia

Into an Ocean ... 45
Jungle ... 46
Just in Case ... 47
Just Like Yesterday ... 48
Last Flutter ... 49
Last Plea ... 50
Last Seal ... 51
Letter to Deaf Eyes ... 52
Lies ... 53
Line Upon Their Years ... 54
Little Lives ... 55
Masquerade ... 56
Mother ... 57
My New Home ... 58
Nothing Less ... 59
Old Bones in the Forgotten City ... 60
Old Fools ... 61
Once Upon a Forest ... 62
Opus Mundi ... 63
Pain? Not! ... 64
Pulling it in ... 65
Raindrops in My Head ... 66
Rebuilding the Thread ... 67
Sacred Bone Yard ... 68
Scent of the Ancient Ball ... 69
Silent Walls ... 70
Skeleton Man ... 71
Sleeping Next to Her Name ... 72
Street Muse ... 73
Supermarket Dreamer ... 74
The Death Before ... 75
The Last Line ... 76
The Taste of Fog ... 77
They Put it in a Box ... 78
Thief ... 79
Tickled in Death ... 80

To the Rhythm of a Dream ... 81
Touching the Ghost ... 82
Under a Golden Blanket ... 83
Unnamed ... 84
Virgin Land ... 85
Waiting for an End ... 86
White World ... 87
Words in Silence ... 88

Author Profile ... 89

In Absentia

In Absentia

A Pile of Bones

Odd couple they stand near a pile of regrets
heads bowed their hands cannot quite reach
yet the tingling increases as energy moves.

Heaped like a warm fir of a past Christmas night
those naked limbs seem to live a strange parody
at play with the memories of lives they once owned.

The glow of the ancient blaze dormant
makes like a chapel consecrated to worship eternity
witnesses they remain quiet as they ponder a purpose.

Still the emanating recollection permeates their essence
and they vanish in a fiery shower of lost destinies
while the army of skeletons continues its lifeless dance.

Would-be makers of infinite worlds, shall they continue
on their stroll through the valleys, forgotten by the giants
or share in the treasures offered by these unlikely benefactors?

Perhaps they will pursue as they do into the evening fires,
the present chapter of a story without a fertile oasis
they too, bones of moments they could not truly cherish.

In Absentia

Balancing into Life

Running to the end of the Earth he would never find
he stands at the edge of a dangerous abyss
to ponder upon a past he could hardly recall.

Life had deserted the warming slopes of a mountain
painted it seems by an impressionist in search of canvas
carved by a cubist unable to reconcile with beauty.

Still he braved the gusts of an evening breeze
arms extended as if ready to take flight into the unknown
eyes shut to feel the hidden secrets of the stony walls.

He could plunge to a certain demise to uncover reality
invited guest through the many gates of this jagged earth
knowing well the infinite peace was within his reach.

Soaring among the layers of a mysterious stratosphere
he passed through the golden cliffs of a last dusk
to be taken into the warm embrace of his final cradle.

Breaking Away

Take those limbs and tear them apart
give them away to the needy
for love, for pain, for a breath come at last.

Explode the tears, vanish the soul
grab at those insides feed them to the dogs
shed the juices of vague sweetness and steel.

Twigs in a game of poker for the destitute
trap the heart, squeeze it in the fatal vise
slowly moving between galaxies and destinies.

Capture the breath in the infinite cosmos
dim its light and crush its last hope
it is time to break this life in two.

In Absentia

Brown Bags

Armed with a last image of a founding father
dragging a leg dressed in borrowed denims
his gaze may be that of a serial killer.

Wednesdays mimic every one of his Sundays
the hourglass might freeze upon an ungodly hour
the neon open sign his only anchor on time.

No word is necessary behind the unkempt hair
the teenager eager for a wage and a date
fulfills for him the usual order, an icy can in a paper bag.

At the gait of a ghost the skeletal apparition exits
a feeble bell greets his departure with great glee
the clueless attendant returns to his mop.

Trucks roar by in hurricanes of diesel fumes
a common sight for this relic of another man's life
his back to the wall he lights up his death.

Testimonial fixture to the a-temporal tragedies
the creature will stand there yet in the rehearsed dusk
the brown paper bag at his feet, casualty of his own being.

In Absentia

Calling in Silence

This is a lucky place
thought I as I sat in obscurity.

I recall no beginning
can fathom no likely exit.

I am simply with a vision
housed in the noble envelope
a treasure uncertain of its form
gently inviting to the traveler.

Senses beyond the earthly realm
shedding the obsolete particles
the finality of all dreams
now with certainty at hand.

This is a fancy world
knew I as I began to fade in eternity.

I now step forward in mere imagination
at last entangled in the blissful call
of a voice universal only to my name
and I lay myself to rest upon infinity.

Chest of Riches

Vagabond on unwritten paths
he saunters heavy leaden.

Facing high blizzards in rags
he might be an errant ghost.

On a journey begun within deep darkness
in search of stars he holds a sacred light
within a chest sized for a grandest myth.

Haggard beneath the weight of a thousand
dreams broken under the yoke of fears
a step yet ahead he dares not rise a gaze.

Another horizon has come to meet the gait
of this traveler in search of a common destiny.

A different sun will set this eve against the silhouette
so strange, and a heaving breast will sigh once more.

There lies his hope gently awaiting
the soft kiss upon a virgin brow.

The cask is heavy with the treasures amassed and
will be opened at last at the feet of the muse
offering of a life's quest to honor its precious source.

In Absentia

Child Yet

They say you must play a part
upon the burning boards of a life
far above days to never really be.

It is an act performed by amateurs
until the final curtain call
in the dark corners of forgotten hopes.

Glaring at costumes worn by a fall
faded within the fibers of another time
the shape of a marionette becomes a statue.

The sketch of a being spirals in its prison
hesitating between a swing and a slide
on the playground of an apocalyptic eve.

This thespian bows under the boos
for his limbs refuse to grow
as he yet laughs and pirouettes away.

Gesture for a forgetting realm
penniless fool on a barren stage
his audience leaves in disbelief.

He is the man who neglected to become
a shadow of the giant awaiting backstage
alone like a child among aging generals.

In Absentia

Christmas in Barbed Wire

Gas of mustard seeds in a muddy grave.
The fizz of copper cones steady as the rain.
The fire in his fingers soon will calm the heart
as the lids will close on the shameful spectacle.
Wire of thorns among the shriveled roses.
A torrent of red and gray will flow near the boots.
Reflected by a sad moon full of grief, of anger.
So many hearts stopped in wait of a sound.

The commotion returns as a stone hits metal
with a soft thump mixed of silence and prayers.
Lids open onto blue, and green, and gray, and black.
Droplets venture upon the soot carving deep crevasses.
On the ruined faces of lives not yet loved a moment
and the tears, too, cry in certain agony
as they mirror the sorrow of a thousand spirits
still holding on to a vague nothingness in moonlight.

Gas of mustard seeds, a copper piece in the flesh.
Dearest memories of hours never spent.
Of a time frozen somewhere in irreverence
along a river that forgot to run its course.
Standing dark against the black sky, shapeless,
a man, dressed in mud, fleshy matter, and a steel hat
looks for his soul somewhere on the field,
seeks the light of a life which ran away

When he could not look, when he was not allowed,
they bought it for nothing, but a pile of bones
found in a hole where he thought they traded his
in the desolation of a world never completed
Home, he dies, the shell of a war that never burst.
The shell of a man who remained a boy of twenty.
At fifty-six he dies of sweet gas of mustard seeds
and copper gifts from another, for a Christmas that never was.

Collapse

I watched the ladder collapse,
rungs rotten to the core,
breaking like twigs in a hurricane.

It once aimed for the skies,
fresh of ancestral lumber,
smiling to the stars above at peace.

It seemed to journey to infinity,
as if jettisoned by a mystical force,
living each day in grandiose ecstasy.

And there it stood, its head in the clouds,
hoping for an eternity
read in novels of old romances.

Nonchalant in the face of suffering,
ignoring the arrogance of the world,
it knew the joys of the innocent.

In Absentia

Crannied Heart

There is just a little crack on the wall
dried on the edges, pink inside,
and still wet with the semblance of a thick nectar
where she rests her thoughts so lightly.

It was but a few memories ago
darkness prevailed on the steps below
to trip up a sweet dream of perfect hours;
a blink from warn sunshine to icy stone.

It is but a fissure on the frame of a soul
warning that a light flickers in sweetest life
flame easily smothered in windless moments
perhaps to lay down what is left of a passion.

Too soon today, the trap not set in doom,
she arises yet again, a grunt, then a grin;
a little crack on the heart the child rests
her soul on a chest her home once again.

In Absentia

Dreams of the Dying

Bright with the life to come,
she looked up with a soft smile
holding the hand of her personal giant.

Her white dress floating above the earth,
comfortable in the gentle embrace,
she stood by him as a ghost.

Hazy memories of unfinished wishes,
like a cloud in the midst of a sublime aura,
persist in the solid waking hours.

Tales of romances never written:
icy alcoves on this side of the night,
torrid evenings in a secretive desert.

Dozing under a fading neon tube,
restless between two worlds,
he owns the gift of passionate eternity.

In Absentia

Elegance

Milky Ways surrounding cream
atop a sweet nectar,
simplicity in a unique singularity.

Atoms sing to their twins
making more than a melody,
flashes of lightning intimate.

Tethers unseen attached in eternity.
They speak a mysterious tongue;
a glue of milk and honey.

Celebration lights in a merry-go-round.
Ferris wheels at great velocities.
Strange creatures comes to life.

The story begins again, so fluid,
a torrent flowing to abysmal seas
of pure joy so loud it seems to scream.

Making a universe, child to a beginning,
a simple elegant evening gown in space.
Life once more to the scale of secret treasures.

In Absentia

Eternity in a Vise

I remember you from another time.
I was so much like you then,
awaiting the grand opportunity
to come along, to walk beside you!

I can still imagine the place.
Though undefined, it was in the spheres.
A bed of clouds and sweet nectar,
it was just a matter of when!

A speck in the universe was you.
No larger was I then.
A hovering electron of light,
I saw you in your little black dress!

Insignificant in a world of giants,
we moved along with the waves of creation;
parallel until finally we met
in a persistent explosion of senses!

And now we hold eternity in a vise
on the infinite path traced for us.
I will not forget the first time I saw you
and dreamed of you in that little black dress.

In Absentia

Exorcised

Enough he said, as he looked into the glass
spying the reflection filled with horror,
the portrait of a once young man hovering.
If only he could shatter the glass with a glance.

Walking in the dark alley, pursued by a shadow,
he cowers in the corner in an attempt to flee again
before the obscurity swallows him;
but it persists, chasing without mercy.

Sleeping another day, dreams become nightmares.
A voice, his without a doubt, screams at him.
A dialogue ensues, an argument possibly to the death,
yet no blood is shed; life continues without hope.

Enough he screamed as he awakened from Hades
a demon on his back, relentless in its quest .
The same self, frightened, lone, full of bile.
If only he could trample on its forked tongue.

He opens his eyes to the frozen image.
It laughs as he attempts to shut his ears to the cacophony.
He turns around and finds a giant haunting his soul.
The skin crawls yet he cannot escape the odious shape.

Running down the eerie corridors lined with tentacles,
he finds a maze without exits echoing of terrifying mockery.
Trapped within a self he has come to abhor,
he seeks a cross to bear; a fountain to regain sanity.

Yet, the vise tightens upon the fragile heart.
Exhausted, he slows his course and collapses on the fire.
Wishing for a single instant of freedom, he fails
and the shroud, his earthly home, engulfs him anew.

Explorer

Explorer, machete in hand and ignorant,
greener than the pines facing him now,
he must find a way to paradise at once
but the pillars are dense as a prison wall.

Squinting through the wilderness forward,
considering exclamations of joy, fearfully
he takes a step and begins to cut to and fro.
Weeds fight viciously back, relentless again.

Wild is the forest of thorns and darkness
attempting to repel this innocent intruder.
Dry of impossible tears all streams have expired.
He comes to a crawl in the remaining mud of river beds.

Pushing forth the last threatening reeds,
the hope is for a moment of rest in the green pasture.
Refreshing in a marsh, friendly echoes of familiar voices
give life again to flowers of a renewed spring.

Perhaps at last he may find the strength to stand
embraced within the warmth of a new home,
mirror image of his very soul's glistening fibers,
friend, mother, oasis and castle all the same.

In Absentia

Farewell

Do I want to see you again?
You who tortured my soul so,
who desired, it seems, only my end.

Could this be my punishment,
in all eternity to meet your gaze again?
You whose eyes are empty sockets.

Will I choose my friends thereafter,
find the warmth of their hearts eternal,
or be forced to feel your glacial presence?

Is rest to be the lot of an old frame,
to retain the image precious of a life
made of the mere glory of modest days?

May I be allowed to expel the aching fibers?
Spew them out as they wish to only rot an old carcass,
and rebuild the temple, sole home to a mortal self,

finding peace at last with all other departed,
who relentlessly follow the eternal path
of an Angelique destiny.

Fashioning a Friend

She caresses the storm ,
gently reclining upon a cloud,
weary of the loneliness she wears.

Flashes streak a threatening darkness,
tracing messages to a dream.
Warmth rises in the deep.

She ponders a creation,
a picture anchored in her imagination
to fashion a fancy she may someday hold.

Cumuli move on to a crawl.
She smiles as they embrace her curves.
A tingling emerges through her pores.

The vast blue of her gaze on fire,
her body acknowledges the ecstasy.
In a moment she will birth the friend.

Her palms warm of the original energy.
Moisture is the nectar of future existence
as before her, Atlas stands to greet his maker.

Fashioning Eternity

Fluid with the power of a Pacific
tsunami pillaging into the depths.
something travels to a destiny.

The waters are frigid, almost solid,
where eyes search for safety
upon a ground known of none.

They appear, classic dancers twirling into space.
Light as if only their souls pirouetted,
enveloped in the arms of the waves.

They may be ancient giants of the oceans,
singing melodies old as the universe,
journeying to their holy grounds.

They will be of indestructible stone,
marble with gentle strikes of pink and blue,
fashioned by the intentional elements around.

It may be the adventure of eons,
gifted of a heavenly destination upon the shore,
when two will reach and gaze into the other's eyes.

Duo, standing tall atop the new galaxy,
they will remain until again they sublime
to be the same, and move on to the eternal realm.

In Absentia

Fear of the Light

I remember the lightning
a little too well;
and the thunder rolling
still in my ears.

Hard rain, cold as ice,
on a tiny little back.
Two miles on a bike,
from third grade, all alone

You taught me to ride,
then you let me go.
Another right of passage,
and yet still a little failed.

Under the crushing skies,
hoping to survive,
to make it home one more time
under disbelieving eyes.

God looked down and smiled,
of course he made it all okay,
even as I crossed the power lines,
and lightning exploded above.

But I didn't ride that day;
I walked under the threat;
My school bag soaked through and through,
and I cried, or was it just hail?

In Absentia

Feeding the Monsters

Imagine cutting through the trap of that aching cage,
ripping skin and bone to take out the rusty machine;
to softly place it on the tray, so desired by the ravenous one.

Offer the warm mass still titillating to the kind hands
and let them hold it near the loving lips.

Let them massage past pains with warm palms
gentle providers of life, as she gives so compassionate a gaze.

Close those eyes to a present made of many perils,
so you may feel her as she touches your very life within.

There is no need to keep the flesh inside the ivory prison.
Safety does not come from the privacy of those cold walls.
It is time, indeed, to feed it to the world hungry for a respite.

Risk it all in the ultimate meekness of the humble lamb.
Lower your glance to await the penalty for innocence
and come to life through the gift of elegant suffering.

Final Talk

We never really knew his age.
Dressed in the weathered leather of years,
he lay lost in the thoughts of decrepit bones.

Absent from the ongoing traffic of hurried feet,
he seemed deaf now to the shaking clamors
echoed through endless corridors.

We sat with him for another celebration,
hoping he would return from his trance.
Seeking comfort in the other, we sighed.

He was engaged in an invisible dialogue,
incapable of breaking from the moment
I know now he was planning for a long journey.

In the sweet silence of his last domain,
I saw him resting a thoughtful mind aglow
upon the shoulder of his eternal friend at last.

In Absentia

Fingerprints on Another Light

What might remain in a distant future,
of the delicate touch upon my door,
volatile finger prints taken by a breeze at dusk.

Footsteps light as those of a gleeful doe,
mindful of dangers in the uncertain forest,
she glides to the outside on a pathway to safety.

Furtive, the fragile apparition may vanish
when a call goes to catch a glimpse of a gaze,
precious to capture the sole moment for tomorrow.

The flash, in deep complicity an eternal treasure,
is the conduit to her smiling soul, wink to the universe.
He cherishes the visitation and lives on.

First Day

He stood at the mouth of a burning Earth
watching the molten rock flow to the ocean
of flames slowing to another landscape.

His feet trembled in unison with the motion
of changes. Wrinkles of youth appeared
below the surface of an emerging world.

Unsure of his own being, he contemplated
the moment, which may be his last,
newborn in a world of chaos and perils.

All around, the earth roared with impatience
growling as if Satan himself sought an escape
from the furnaces of his fiery home.

A peak rose slowly seeking cooler climes,
a haven for the safety of the lone adventurer
still, as an icy storm came to be for the first time.

Sovereign of a most hostile kingdom, he would wait
for the deliverance of a fertile imagination
to create lands full of unending majesty.

Alone between the infinite spaces of a new realm,
the wishes of his fragile bones began to ooze
into a domain where his heart might beat at last.

Flight of the Swallows

Her body spoke, the soul was silent
far too often; but he knew,
in all the pain, the heart was quiet
and it hurt, but he knew.

Four scores and five years;
flesh and bones made up the words.
The truth remained in the shadow,
though magnificent it was.

Oceans of tears it shed and caused;
the body that suffered crippled the mind,
and then it was silent.

The pain cried, and burnt the flesh,
to be reborn.
And he knew all along,
the beautiful one that came back for him.

One quarter score passed.
She waited in the corner.
He knew always what no one else did.
And now they live again.

Two friends free, swallows
of the barn who one evening
bid me farewell, in the sweet flutter
of their wings.

When the body spoke, the soul was silent,
but he knew her heart all along.

Floating

Strolling at noon on a precious day,
when ghosts hover to a favorite dive,
he bumped elbows with a girl in white.

The zenith stood guard above misery
throwing flames into his indecent gaze
for he must not dare to confront the heavens.

Black souls danced arm in arm
walking in a deathly cadence
until the bell again rang for order.

She did not belong in this ghastly crowd,
her body smiling with the aura of ideals;
a promise she vanished in a private realm.

The absent-minded saunterer attempted to follow her
beyond the glaring windows;
a bright world in this indecent nightmare.

Her vision invited the stranger one last time;
but he could only remain by the gate of horror
to see her disappear within the world she saved.

Free

It sounds like a pebble in a tin can,
resonates with the memories
of perhaps another.

Looking around, spinning again,
even the clouds are deaf
to my desperate query.

Senses entangled in an odd message,
images I once printed
on the walls of that old soul,
bicker with the scents of the land.

Taking another aimless step
the ground fails me as always;
of course I slip farther down the alley.

What I once tasted as a child;
a tart of berries and apples;
touches the unknown membranes
in the next world to welcome me.

There is a tingling in my brain,
a joyful escapade form this realm.
I may be free yet again.

In Absentia

Frozen Features

They all recall days of gentle spirits,
friends and kin alike, not long ago
when she glided upon her carefree ways.

No hall remained empty upon her passage
when her deep aura left a print
onto the walls of brick, stone and diamond.

A harsh season rose above the horizon
too frigid for the feeble limbs;
little girl in shock before the highest peaks.

Somewhere below the gray, she knew happiness.
Now buried beneath the weight of massive memories,
she suffers in every crushed fiber.

In silence she pleads for a better moment,
praying for the message traced within the flesh
to be known of those who cry nearby.

Far too solemn for the years, she is as ice
frozen as once was stone of this earth,
paralyzed below the mere fears of being.

She used to dance with infinite freedom
making sounds of laughter to echo forevermore.
Inside the shell she screams to find herself again.

Solid in a present she never sought.
The time will come for her to arise at last.
Kind soul you are missed in this darkening realm.

In Absentia

Gambling with My World

Playing with dice,
throwing the cubes
on a concave table,
they cried their joy.

A complete deck,
aces, and queens
dealt on a grassy
plate, they yell.

A bet, an ante,
a few heavy coins
of silver, gold,
nickels and dimes,

and the universe is born,
for it must come to life;
stars, galaxies, planets
and all, they pray.

It has been cast now;
destinies drawn in the skies;
lives gambled away, and
they sing praises.

In Absentia

Grace Undercover

There is blood in the grooves of a dried-up soil.
Our ground still screams from memories fast gone.
Life ends again where a seed was to grow.

Mountains neighbor the deep canyons next door.
Tightrope walkers hesitate to take on the promenade
considering abysses as they stand atop a chimney to the core
of a living body of molten desires for an unknown future.

The traitorous journey will continue perhaps
until we open our eyes and trust, blind to the light,
into a final leap over the obscured depths of dying souls.

In Absentia

Grounded

Darkness prevails once again.
It is late at night in the haunted house;
the swallows too have gone to sleep,
as rain has become too heavy for flight.

Staying warm is a difficult task,
when fire reaches only the bones.

I choose to live in my head by this rainy day,
to find a semblance of comfort and safety,
away from a dense reality frozen in time.

Memories crowd space, many too distant,
oppressing the stranger I have become,
in a home mine where the sage remains,
hovering in a gentle embrace so loving.

Staying inside one's soul is the answer,
while the pain seeks an opening,
to leave a scar deep to the heart,
and the rain seems as hail from below.

In Absentia

His Kingdom for a Touch

At the furthermost corner of the curb,
contemplating a new tear in the soiled denim,
no thought crosses that aging soul.

Without raising an eye he sees the world
under the reddish shade of a ravenous pyre;
if only the dying warmth could give him life.

A little boy once sat where he now dies.
In colorful giggles he played with a girl.
A dream fading with his aching bones.

He touches his wrists where she held him,
a vague memory of anticipated moments
when they simply embraced in secret.

Soon the frigid air of the night will enlace
this abandoned mass of wasted fancies
to crush the fragile remains of her image.

Alone the rotting statue will endure
his kingdom dilapidated to the last hope
for a kind touch in the self-imposed exile.

In Absentia

The body rests in an ocean of down and silk
stirring from time to time into a second of life,
a subtle jerk, and peace again in a soft glow.

To the other, she stays in a gentle slumber,
refuge from a time so near, barely forgotten,
she seems to be seeking an answer.

A quick twitch of a lip and she slips once more;
inside, time has ceased to hold on tight,
she has attained freedom from all boundaries.

The moment has come, so eagerly awaited;
the taste of all senses now belongs to her,
as she roams in a realm alike the Milky Way.

Hovering between this Earth, and another,
her soul collects pieces from another ether,
making up memories of lives never lived.

Tomorrow glimpses will return, and in awe,
she will wonder as she catches sight
of those instants now so real, in patches.

She knows soon again there will be a time
when all limits collapse and then the owner
of infinities already encountered, she will be.

In Dali's World

What is a humanoid to do
when the body is trapped
in Dali's fluid memories?

The thoughts dissipate in colored
molasses, uncertain lines to distant
horizons lost in infernal scenery.

It knows somewhere in time exist
the limbs of motion but it remains
blind in an eerie cosmic gaze.

It might saunter in the grayish meadow,
venture under the harrowing rains
of steel traveling at the speed of comets.

The creature wishes it could be
whole at last under the brush of life,
but the universe is persistent in its denial.

A nebula, essence of an unborn soul;
mere idea of what may someday become
an unwilling shape shifter it will continue
to hover in its eternal search for completion.

In Absentia

In the Valley of the Gods

I have walked through the devil's garden,
seeking nothing but the beauty of this world,
feeling the remaining heat of a scorching eve.

I have driven a carriage upon a road forgotten of this age,
encountering the oddities of a future not yet made,
questioning whether I must go on to live.

I have plunged into the entrails of the earth,
following curves into a vertiginous certainty,
oblivion at every turn, a terrifying absolution.

Yet I stopped in contemplation of a world above.
Into a deep night I swam guided by a rising current
onto a path made of a molten world to another day.

Alone in the midst of growing peaks I knelt,
as darkness fell upon my soul in an explosion of stars,
one at last with all, sighing as I greeted the cosmos.

In Absentia

Into an Ocean

There was once a little girl perhaps a boy, certainly
a thing that lived and giggled in the soft breeze of morning.

The thing traveled, for it was its destiny,
downward to meet a friend or two and make a family.

The thing was scared a little at first, they say
rolling down, casting down, crashing down, and again.

Then it joined forces with the unknown, the new,
the same as it was in the mirror of another day.

It saw an odd thing, made of steel, and wood, and
two-legged machines pushing and pulling upon the forest.

There was a journey to make, so on the thing went.
Shiny in the daily star, it made hues of a million shades.

It crashed against a wall at the speed of another time
eyes opened to prevent a destiny meant for another.

Soldier in an infinite army of two, she continued on her way
shaping a world with gentle hands, artist of many worlds.

He saw villages, and towns, and cities of strange brethren
going on to a future to last beyond the realms of his country.

She gave him a thing also to take into his wandering soul.
He let something new emerge from the mountain he once was.

Behind them, they left a vein throbbing from the calm unknown
so they could take a bow and sleep
in the midst of the grand creation.

Jungle

If you were a jungle
I would brandish the machete,
cut through the vines, numb the thorns
and venture into the dark unknown.

If you were a castle
I would run to the drawbridge,
seek the steel curtains
and part my way through the thick walls.

If you were a garden
I may plea for a chance to enter,
inhale your infinite perfumes
and let you carry me on to your secrets.

If you were catacombs or a graveyard
I may mourn the sadness of my kin,
change a spring suit for a shroud
and disappear into your infinite abyss.

If you were a desert
I might fear the heat of summer dusks,
renounce my wish to pay you a visit
and sleep upon your sands.

But you are an ocean
deep with the mystery of numerous lives lost
and I merely shiver awaiting your call
to surrender to the rapture of your voice.

Just in Case

He awoke at a time without hour,
threw a leg to the floor as the morning before,
mechanical as the machine of so many dawns,
just in case this day something new could happen.

He dared look into the glass for new signs of hope
finding once again the smooth spot of his youth
and walked to the room where a fresh aroma brewed,
just in case he found something to do.

He ventured into the world so little changed,
a fresh Saturday on the eve of another summer,
crowds already seeking the excitement of festivals,
just in case there could be a story to recount on Sunday.

He had spied an ad he could not resist,
gathered all his thin courage to walk into the cathedral
and piled the bounty in a glorious artificial pouch,
just in case another week would grace him with a little life.

Every second he contemplates fragments of a world
he has known for weeks and years without end
and goes about a routine he has long forgotten,
just in case he could live to burst into bliss.

In Absentia

Just Like Yesterday

Watching the greens spreading to oceans
the virus conquered beyond the horizon.

Wheeled white carcasses they race,
maggots seeking yet another rotten meal,
they slalom on the manmade scars.

Shiny tops, rusty joints, arched skeletons,
they act as knights errant with their swords
shining in the eagerly awaiting lightning.

They roar at the speed of death
bombarding the living with dying anger.

Half blind zombies, they seem aliens to the realm,
searching within little holes in the planet,
under the jealous glare of hungry gophers.

There was once a time when they mattered,
riding the highways of existence to the bank,
but the spark has dimmed in the glazed pupils.

Pretending to play for one last adventure,
they push on the gas to the eighteenth.

Leaving a trail of empty aluminum behind,
meek bracelet celebrating their earthly mother,
they crawl into rivers of contaminated milk.

They are just like Ebola these odd mounts;
plague upon a noble land tortured by the sadness
of those who seek yet a pathway to another destiny.

In Absentia

Last Flutter

Raindrops dying on the Pacific
struggle to be remembered
far below.
They make no sound
at the bottom of the abyss;
the echo of their minute lives
never lost to infinity.

Fallen from his haven branch,
playful to his last breath,
the newly born winged angel,
never to be the giant in his father's pupil,
stares to the stars
hoping for a last chance
as his heart slows to be still.

So many hearts lie about the land,
shining in the icy drops,
teased by a cruel moment
they flutter unseen,
soon to be crushed by the wanderer.
Innocent, they plead for an embrace
to merely cry in oblivious silence.

In Absentia

Last Plea

I have counted the years on the hourglass
watching sand flow as if rusted blood.

Spring has come to mock eternal winters,
always victorious in this eerie land.

Below my house a lake sleeps full of tears,
still, beneath a thin veil of bluish steel.

My walls covered with the markers of decades,
I hug the wind full of its icy embrace.

This plea may be the last offered to the cosmos,
a heaven where old friends meet again.

Soon it will be too late for this earthly bliss,
but an instant is all I fancy closing my eyes.

Come and bid me farewell upon the slab
the grip of death will charm as does your soul.

In Absentia

Last Seal

There is a velvety place with the sweetness of nectar,
a valley made for the gods where none is welcome;
remembering of births, forecasting wondrous climes,
a bed of young leaves of grass and budding blossoms.

Safe haven, no less than heaven in every season
to rest one's intimate dreams upon the restful pillow,
into an impossible death from the gentle roots of a mother.

Exploring the deep discovery between those mounds,
parting the green curtains softly to the next realm
as a dew settles from the sweet breath of a giant,
there is no more a need to rise but to surrender.

The kiss of life is shared by much more than crimson lips,
as the hollow closes onto this prison of one penitent,
not to be encountered again outside of these marble walls,
the future is sealed in union of vale and conquered intruder.

In Absentia

Letter to Deaf Eyes

Strings flash through the grays above.
Chirps die under the fist of pounding storms
while a star shies away from the dark dawn.

Hours of impossible dreams come to a halt
under the feeble flame of a forgotten lamp.
Wild locks wet with flowing pains, he aches.

It is a familiar scene of hope and despair.
An aura, shaped like a shade on wishes, falls
upon the letter begun when he could still inhale.

Like blood to the rivers of forgotten slaughters,
the ink traces a story upon the velvet sheet
prolonging the comfort of a refuge found in the alcove.

The future suddenly brighter, enlightens the darkish orbs
as his soul screams through the cosmos under the quill.
The same eternal plea to echo on, to touch its goal.

There is a warm spark titillating deep below
and he smiles for a moment embracing the form
of the apparition who does not yet know she is.

In Absentia

Lies

They choose words to speak of the morrow
telling ancient stories of gods and goblins;
images in black and white in a technicolor world.

Artists at the reins of a strange cavalcade,
they race with the determination of giants,
brows frowned upon tales they refuse to tell.

Waving pennants on the sidelines babes cry.
The idols of a recent day have forgotten
promises made by the hearth just last eve.

Crowds weep in unison the agony
of an era devoid of warming hopes,
their bodies crumbling to icy ashes.

Modern knights now pursue their infernal quest
for all things shiny with the weight of riches
as they crush those trusting little dreams.

In Absentia

Lines Upon Their Years

They recall fragile petals crowding their world,
cries of joy as they stepped to the new path,
Pachelbel fading behind the pearly train.

It was as frigid rains in a summer afternoon,
deep grooves upon the slippery asphalt,
lines traced into a joyful future.

Soon, beneath wings of steel, they saw fiery skies
gently gliding to oceans of immense possibilities
into calm luxury of first moments in white satin.

Their history is carved upon the eternal parchment
with laughter, sobs, sighs, moans, groans and screams;
lines between the lives they made in a great domain.

So close now they seem to sleep again,
statues in celebration of common eternities,
mummified by the warmth of their caresses.

Gauzy gazes encircled by the scars of many battles,
they dive into the swirling galaxy they will leave behind,
two comets aimless in their eternal journey to paradise.

In Absentia

Little Lives

Little lives crawl upon the pane of glass at dusk
forgotten on an ice sheen in winter.

Miniature monsters explore mountains of sand
lost in a sea of luxuriant green.

No thought of tomorrow in those carefree souls,
busy at existing for lack of being.

Sensing a breeze, touching a heat, they go on
and return to a start as to an end.

A symphony of crackles surrounds their feet
under a shower of shady rays.

Soon night will come again beneath a dark cloud,
they will ignore the silence of men.

They will continue the endless dialogue of beast
far greater in eternal numbers.

While the rulers of the universe continue to vanish,
one by one, without much of a sound.

Masquerade

It might be terror beneath the fainted masks
for those mobs in search of another moment.

Perhaps they grin in mockery below
makeshift bullet proof suits.

I wonder if they cry within the flesh
as they race to another decaying quest.

What suffering lies inside shrunken entrails
where hearts float without anchorage.

Multitudes wander lost in their cities
bumping into invisible walls.

Their faces pale as if yet departed
bluish veins scar sunken cheeks.

Corpses before they know their fates,
so futile the daily chores.

Thin as tulle, the cloth dissipates
upon the same specter of death.

In Absentia

Mother

He was an explorer of sorts.
Aimless, a vagabond through dense forest.
A babe falling upon the forgotten puddles of winter.
A child, seeking a way home.

A would-be Superman, eagle, soaring to the stratosphere,
he sought an entrance to the forbidden palace
desperate for the connection
back to his own creation.

The sea offered him a fertile land,
mother of mothers, home to the origins
some say, upon a shore the first man landed
but he goes on in search of a golden gate.

Man born of a gentle affair at the height of darkness.
Tadpole, he fights a current to a great secret
as waters of fire bubble about his membrane,
suddenly a flash and it is light.

Wrapped within the eons of the universe,
 his mother cradled in the arms of warm constellations
so small, he finds his domain at last;
infant of apparent infinity.

In Absentia

My New Home

I awoke in a thickest night.
laden with restless dreams.
swimming in the rains of darkness.

Flesh upon satin, my soul burnt
naked to the core, seeking another home,
I may have wiggled as once in the womb.

Discerning the fibers in burgundy ooze,
I closed my eyes to plunge into a future,
as so many dawns before, to a fresh skin.

Near the alcove, a memory lay
defunct on the undertaker's icy tile:
what I had been but hours before.

Snug inside the silk of my cocoon,
every pore came alive with as many sighs,
to deepest sleep I surrendered this life.

Nothing Less

I walk through a desert land
cliché of all that has been.
crowded with infested mobs.
the walking shells nothing but ghosts.

Yet I refuse to settle for less
than all there is in this realm;
a unity to find the power of wings
and fly away to distant worlds.

To find a living one among these apparitions
I will risk every particle;
exposing a core to complete annihilation;
so per chance I may become complete.

Searching for those lost atoms,
I seek the irresistible pull of another,
wandering as I am upon uncertain paths
to merge in infinite ecstasy.

In Absentia

Old Bones in the Forgotten City

Odd couple, they stand near a pile of regrets
heads bowed, their hands cannot quite reach
yet the tingling increases as energy moves.

Heaped like a warm fir of a past Christmas night,
those naked limbs seem to live a strange parody
at play with the memories of lives they once owned.

The glow of the ancient blaze, dormant,
makes like a chapel consecrated to worship eternity.
Witnesses, they remain quiet as they too ponder a purpose.

Still the emanating recollection permeates their essence
and they vanish in a fiery shower of lost destinies
while the army of skeletons continues its lifeless dance.

Would-be makers of infinite worlds, shall they continue
on their stroll through the valleys, forgotten by the giants;
or share in the treasures offered by these unlikely benefactors?

Perhaps they will pursue, as they do into the evening fires,
the present chapter of a story without a fertile oasis,
they too, bones of moments they could not truly cherish.

In Absentia

Old Fools

The bus will be late again this Sunday.
Under the century mist on a cold winter bench
old fools must wait, their gaze upon a gate
to a paradise, invisible to the passers-by.

The city sleeps still in a shroud of oblivion.
Lives have slipped into their temporary tomb,
worn to pieces by the inferno of infinite routines,
while last trees cry dying leaves upon the icy pavement.

The two might sleep for a little while:
he holding tight onto the shiny tank;
she dragging on a grayish cloud of ash;
ancient as the traditions graved on monuments.

Unseen, living in the wrinkly bubble of their age,
they seek the hesitant gaze of the other.
Memories built upon the fresh bones of infants,
a smile, shy as a fleeting moment, escapes the universe.

They laugh no more. To the keen eye of the observer
the flesh has fallen off the crackling frames
leaving senseless messages of passed lives
upon the pavement, welcoming to their shameless survival.

The decades have built fortresses around their secrets;
shriveled breasts kindly placed onto an altar
still beat with the passion of a single score.
Carrying too many years to count, they love for all time.

In Absentia

Once Upon a Forest

He lived the story of a thousand years;
wanderer in a quest for another wilderness.

Often the search ended on the edge
of a city surrounded by ancient walls.
Hero, hoping for a denouement,
he would just fall to his knees.

The secrets of a life to be, their prisoner
a lone knight errant touching the frigid stone.
Listening to the pulse of a stranger
he seems to rest, at last, almost alive.

Parting the leaves of the antique forest,
hoping for a smile, he teases at the gate
while a storm unleashes its ultimate warning
upon the frail frame shivering to a crumble.

There, in the stillness of eternity
he will continue to dream,
his fingers holding the chapters revealed.

Opus Mundi

They dance on a line like acrobats.
Artists of many languages, they paint
in the air the symphony of unending days.

In a tremendous unity they conquer
a world made at the size of a musical staff.
Humble and meek, they inscribe a song
on walls immemorial, building posterity
witnesses to an epoch never to be dismissed.

Chorus, chorale, orchestra, ballerinas, all,
musicians in their own right, composers
in their sleep, actors in their wake, magicians
their creation comes alive with the wand.

Precarious existences speaking to the unknown
draw their faith in the firmament with stars.
Winged angels, they make our dreams real
with endless breaths so very deep.

Brushstrokes, so wide, splatter on the canvas.
So much force, vibrant colors with pulsating beats.
Notes mix a drunken alphabet; they remember
Praxiteles, Leonardo, Ludwig, Andy, and more.

The realm made of all senses, their true country.
For never will they rest, their work everlasting.
Artists, whose gift is the touch of God, they carve
on space and time the glory of the infinite second.

In Absentia

Pain? Not!

Suffering in the dolce vita of yesteryear. We part the world
gleeful within the pain, made like the softest blanket of stars.
We implode into infinite knowledge to the depths of wisdom.

Lying on a bed of molten earth, we find a soothing river,
infinite in its motion to a sea of gentle passion,
holding those extremities with gazes of cutting ice.

Paradox of contradictions, we find peace in the bodily wars,
struggling through puzzlement to discover only answers
to the many queries we never dare make in earnest.

Brittle bones crackle like dying fires at the bottom of the Pacific,
but spirits know no horror from the crushing of their enemies.
Watery diamonds, they slip through the cold grasps of monsters.

Heroes born of a fleeting flash in a dim passion, we die
perishing upon the jagged shore of the unforgiving sea,
never apart when our bodies are severed from gentle souls.

Pain? Not now! It is the impossible dream of the eternal foe
perched on a thorny nest upon the dark tower of frigid ivory.
He imagines the fear he can no longer fester in the meek.

We vanish indeed! Our limbs torn, hearts broken, eyes pierced.
Victorious in oblivion, we will reign in the ultimate dominion
for our sufferance is but the spice of the meals we crave.

In Absentia

Pulling it in

I have walked in the valley of
many desolations surrounded by
crumbling giants of dust and sand.

Rivers flowed to their origin
at the center of this collapsing verse.

I stood on the bank of asphalt torrents,
scarlet arteries of infinite memories,
and saw nothing but eternally lost souls.

The ground below moved in unison with
a strange symphony of deep earthly groans.

It was like a vortex pulling it all in;
source of all energies finally reconciled,
revealing the mysteries of never-ending births.

So fortunate I found myself in the center
and understood at long last my simple purpose.

Raindrops in My Head

I like the sound the rain makes as it rattles in my skull,
'tis better than cob webs, dust and empty spaces.

Old house, crumbling temple water damaged altar;
the seals are weak with a pressure so intense.

Light to storm, neurons flow electrifying the air;
a hurricane dares be born and swirl around fearless.

The ego becomes dizzy as hinges screech in agony.
Doors slam on truths and lies alike, then silence.

Another drop, larger, vaporizes its predecessor
and the walls become slippery to memories.

A sweet breeze pushes the waves aside, clearing the way
to an unlikely sunshine, to the hope of eternal moonshine.

Echoes arise in the sphere emptied of ancient filth.
Tomorrow will be another day for glory, love and hate.

In Absentia

Rebuilding the Thread

Remembering the skill of the fate,
I contemplate a light beyond the stars
begging for the miracle of a mysterious power.

It has been too long since I began roaming the seas,
an unanchored ship in the midst of endless storms
floating above perilous abysses of a thick blackness.

I can still catch a glimpse of the fibers
ripped by a heartless jolt at an instant of joy;
they seem alive with an instinct to rejoin.

Somewhere on the other side of these quicksands
the severed half remains in desperate wait,
decaying on the stone of a deserted harbor.

I face aft as I aim to discover a brighter form.
A hand begging for a touch however brief,
warm with the desire to reconnect forevermore.

In Absentia

Sacred Bone Yard

Looking for parts to upgrade old chassis,
hand in hand, they stroll in search of a miracle.
A crow recites the song of his forefathers
perched on the trusted rust of yesteryear.

Strange lovers alien to prettier days,
they stare at a would-be sun beyond the storm.
Wearing patches of ongoing hopes they dream
worn out bones unwillingly playing a melody.

Like the old Model T they once drove to the ocean
they fancy a renewal promised on futuristic billboards.
New limbs, a little used perhaps, but never broken
organs made for the universal soldier.

Their shoulders touch to the melting spot
grown like conjoined Siamese legends.
They still imagine the sunset of their parents
when sitting on the porch of endless possibilities.

Hand in hand, they stumble between the rows of cadavers
pressing upon their path into a thicker darkness.
No hearts to be found here, nor any new fantasies
just the eerie sounds of agonizing carcasses.

Not a word is said between those two legends,
their lives finished under a reddish realm.
One more step and it is done as if they had never been
a weak aura remains of those ancient silhouettes.

Soon others will follow the road already taken,
enticed by the gentle pull a forgotten old couple.

In Absentia

Scent of the Ancient Ball

There's a dim-rayed future behind the cracks of the ramparts.
Sounds emanate from the twirling shapes of silken whites,
while the stone burns with the icy flames of the prison.

To be part of this strange ball but a dream in the depths,
inhaling fumes of a past reverie poison or elixir,
aiming to taste what remains of the ghostly dance.

The heavy oaken gate persists in its temerity.
Its lock, rusted, melts into torrents of bloody paste.
No drawbridge will again annihilate the cruel moat.

It is a tower of ivory, mother of pearl, diamond and silver;
treasure for the hungry to be consumed perhaps too late
where she is surrounded by the death-defying maidens.

Centuries go by, she continues in her light genuflection
hands joined in a prayer seeking only communion;
one with all, pure of soul as once of body.

Silent Walls

Glacial in the dead of a brutal summer,
the room is as barren as the undertaker's.

Blinding with flames of sterile light,
it seems flashes enter the broken glass.

Forgotten by all those who may care,
a witness stands statuesque in the doorway.

Not a sound dares penetrate those frigid walls;
nor a scent flavor dawns of puerile springs.

A vacuum to all life, empty as a hollow tomb,
it is the prophesy of an irreparable future.

An otherwise safe room in a grand fortress,
danger reigns there as it recalls a coming death.

Surrounded by the joy of common days,
the void soon will swallow all remaining hope.

Alone, the giant of the obsolete domain
falters near the abyss of an impossible legacy.

Forced to enter the inescapable destiny of oblivion,
the gate stealthily closes upon dire desperation.

In Absentia

Skeleton Man

Joe. I think
I heard his name called at the station
leaning against the post of a rotten frame
a wet cigarette dangling from the crumbling flesh.

Joe, a voice inside echoed
as if a stick figure something like an arm moved
holding a can of the cheapest brew he could afford,
he spat black tar to the wind.

Content in the fumes of a gasoline pump,
Joe, the young man carrying the weight of centuries.
Everyday idle as if it were a choice.
A meaning lost in the smog of dying dawns.

The face engulfed in a graying bush of wild curls.
Eyes sunken in a vain attempt to escape.
The view of a sunset far too distant.
Dreams drawn in an old schoolboy's notebooks.

He rides his old wheels from one corner to the next
braving wind, sleet and hurricanes.
The fading butt in the terrified beak,
he barely remembers when he drove the rusty truck.

A skeleton, barely a reminder of the man he once was,
eaten by smoke, bad beer and the disintegration of his hopes,
he still smiles when answering the question of his purpose.
Joe replies: "It's a living, ain't it?

In Absentia

Sleeping Next to Her Name

Magic happens when a wish is born
lying on the side of an old home,
and a last sigh shakes the world
before night crushes the last spark of daylight.

Miles away from the curves she made,
warmth still vibrates through the membrane
of an ever-moving realm born of her womb.

Closing his mind to futile hours,
skin to wood he does not mind the cold
of the pine tombstone as he drifts
into the living embrace of the vision.

Remembering the life before time began,
curled into the hands of a mother,
he gives all he is to the nurturer
smiling in death as in certain life.

Street Muse

I cannot quite recall the year,
yet I do remember the sounds of fumes.

An electric tram slid by
surrounded by the neon of trendy windows.

Cobblestones reminded walkers of times immemorial
carrying their precious cargo in silk purses.

Could they slow for a moment and live again?
I wondered as I sat in her tremendous shade.

Stranger in the land of plenty,
she looked to the heavens with amazing grace.

Her ritual smile hovering upon those juvenile lips,
she inhaled once more and took another gliding step.

Armed with the joyful bow, she began
singing hallelujahs upon her gentle wings.

In Absentia

Supermarket Dreamer

To the cornucopia of endless feasts
he rushes, giant in the labyrinth,
legitimate hunter of a thriving tribe.

His soul shines with the smiles of destinies,
when he will return to the hearth,
his fists filled with nectars of distant lands.

I saw him once before in the mist,
carrier of gentle thoughts for all,
on a mission to share his modest glee.

Race car driver between the solitary aisles,
the lengthy limbs carefully slalom
between the pillars of this odd temple.

Caretaker of those he nurses with his lifeblood,
he might as well dance on his way to the gates
leaving behind the daily din of this glass palace.

In Absentia

The Death Before

In absolute repose, the aging child stands
atop a landscape forbidden to his kin.
Ethers hover, lost between lives.

The substance of what he may be, lost.
Ghost of a self he may never encounter,
wandering in the midst of contradictory ecstasies.

Does he truly live in the cage of those bones?
Is the pain in the fibers of this time?
Perhaps consciousness has already fainted.

In Absentia

The Last Line

He looked forward to the distant skies
beyond a sea of lead, heavy, as if another earth
with waves made of a paste as molasses.

Perhaps there was hope upon the horizon,
as he collected the abandoned tools of his craft,
pondering the words he should scribe to the winds.

Far without the reach of un undying aim,
a soul dreams of the final message he may conceive,
calling upon eternity to give him a last greeting.

His wish to see the melody that will sing his world,
carved on the hazy mists of endless dimensions;
but moments before he gives an ultimate sigh.

The Taste of Fog

Early morning darkness subsides,
victim to the warming rays of the great master,
boiling dew into a strange golden mist.

I drink the day's gentle potion to eternity,
seeking a flavor unknown in the fields of man,
toasting another success story yet to come.

Forest giants lay their claim to the cup of gold
towering over the wanderer dwarfed in the dawn.
Night creatures recede to their distant dens.

I continue on the familiar path to the silver land,
venturing another taste before it is too late,
for soon this mild curtain will fade into the light.

Carrier of peculiar souls, the fog is still
holding the silence of lives forgotten by the hours.
I take another drop and swallow the essences of infinity.

In Absentia

They Put it in a Box

They put it in a box and said good-bye;
those bipeds in white gowns almost angels
hovering inside the walls of a faded green hue.

Joe, his mother called him and so he remained
until the hands on the clock changed to mush,
hesitant between the classroom and the morrow.

And he sang for no reason at all in a strange tongue
and laughed just because it was gleeful to do so,
always late against the steep curve of the hill.

Glad was Joe just to be with those odd youngsters
across from the gentle soul of a red-headed maiden.
She too looking at the oblong cask of the old schoolboy.

Something just did not work anymore inside the prison.
It was time to go home albeit a little too soon,
for this day he would be early in a timeless realm.

The wheels broke so they replaced them with gold
tried pearls, and the precious metals of alchemists
making a new machine so his life would continue to flow.

It was a week, perhaps a month or a year, but treasures too die.
His sad gaze upon the box, he saw them taking it away
and onto the wings of sleep he caught an eternity made for him.

Joe, they called him, Joe alone with a deep hole in his chest.
They took the old heart he delighted in and teased so lightly
and they put it in a box, and all said good-bye at last.

In Absentia

Thief

At sixteen hundred and a few years, he locked the door;
his room was his domain in the house her family built.

Between the walls white so pure, he dreamed a future;
his mind a maze of visions, ideas and passions.

Through the window a deep meadow smiled in all seasons,
lightning stabbed the air, and shook him to his gentle core.

There, facing the fury of a nature unknown, his refuge
behind him, the powerful anger of the unwilling adult.

At sixteen hundred and twelve more moons, his hand tickled
for the quill, as great rivers wanted to bleed on the velum.

He gave birth to an unlikely field of foreign lands,
a cradle for a sore soul prisoner, fearful of neighbors.

The door remained locked, so she cried mighty and loud,
to be quiet on end, driving him into her personal oblivion;

Soon, he could only see his fleshy envelope and wonder
why so much hate came his way when he cried.

Thief, she could not complete her task, before the door,
punished him for wanting to be alive on the other side.

The little back trembled with thought of the executioner
within the wall of a fortress where she roamed hungry.

Trapped within the puzzling prison of the matron,
under the pained eye of a third, lord emasculate.

He pulled the covers higher, staring at the flashes in heaven,
like yet another dagger hurled from her venomous gaze.

In Absentia

Tickled in Death

Brother of a forgotten Usher, perhaps he drifted.
Particles of an abandoned carcass in a deep crevasse,
he joined the sparkling ballet of quantum stars.

As it had once in the life of another time,
ultimate knowledge stabbed at his very essence
with the ongoing persistence of the infinite.

There was no pain in this anesthetic state,
shrouded as he was within the secrets only he had shared,
feeling from all sides in a realm with no reference.

Expanding as would another universe, he floated now,
energy teasing the fibers freed by the death of a body.
He was tickled to life now, understanding his purpose.

In Absentia

To the Rhythm of a Dream

For centuries, this man has stood atop the galaxy.
I saw him once at the edge of the caldera.
He sat, quietly, contemplating his own soul
written on the walls of the azure, in red
and in orange, and in purple as if a sunset.

He caught a glimpse of a life stilled into eternity
painted by a friend long gone, to Everest or Kilimanjaro
standing as she looked to the world of her kin below,
her bare feet warm with the amorous snows,
above the sky, so close to heaven, her true home.

She saw memories drawn on the clouds by the hand
of a grandfather decades ago teaching a son to draw
by the lake the gleeful fowl in the rite of spring.
Wrinkles filled with the powdery charcoal of blue
and of gray, and of the tones of a grand flight.

The sharp eyes, squinting through the teasing waves
of a mermaid lost in the sweet waters of man;
or the fairy who once took them on a journey
in a land like Eden, not so far from their cabin in the woods,
when they let their hearts slow to the rhythm of a dream.

In Absentia

Touching the Ghost

Trembling digits tend to an invisible form.
Memories of a vision beyond a dark wall.
A dream as true as the life he seeks.

Frightened for perhaps it is but a ghost
the temporary apparition of a glowing mist
still as if too attempting to become flesh.

To touch a star born with the first lights,
his body shivers under the warmth of early dawns.
One more step into the unknown and it will be done.

It may be a ghost all that still remains
for him to join and gently vanish
touching the light essence of his passion.

Under a Golden Blanket

Warrior in his red cape,
he howled at the moon at midday
dreaming of the maiden to rescue.
Middle-school knight with little to lose.
Across the aisle in her spring dress
enthralled by an author's every word
she contemplated the little girl
cuddled in the warm womb of a mother.

A destiny in precious stones
sealed in certainty of what could be theirs.
In black and white they covered the path
under the arbor made of best wishes.
The hourglass began on its course
in a new home made of gentle reason.
It rested comfortably for each day
upon decades solid as eternity.

Chasing a star of honey and other delights
their journey ended beneath a golden blanket;
a field of wheat by a scorching afternoon
spotted in crimson gashes of gory grimaces.
She had smiled until then.
When, with the barrel upon her breast,
she was made the object of monstrosity
to fall in the lone abyss of her lost innocence.

And he, vanquished conqueror, felled
upon the root of budding lives,
protecting with his senseless expiation
the warmth of her last loving words.
A field of infinite birthing nature,
they lay in decay, beneath the depth of space,
victims of unfathomable games
in their monochrome costumes of ecstasy.

Unnamed

A faint spark in the desert once,
as if a glimmering speck of infinite sands,
far from the oasis hope failed to nourish,
she struggled but for a brief moment.

She must have wondered why the light died
in the intense sun of an August drought;
exile among exiles, forgotten of the living,
neglected in a mere instant of joy.

Stilled in infancy, she cried out for help
while images of future dreams and deeds
flashed before the brand-new soul
so much desiring to grow a fertile womb.

But darkness overcame her bluish vision,
blinded by the memories she would never have.
Tears perhaps would have saved her little life
if only her name had been written upon the dune.

In Absentia

Virgin Land

Long ago the tremors ceased;
this land left untouched.

Abandoned to the chiming of slow hours;
a desert grown from ancient vales.

Once fertile grounds to extreme glee
now silent as the coming day of doom.

On islands in the midst of sandy oceans
a gentle touch seems to persevere.

She recalls the better years when winter ices
thawed soft upon her contented breath.

The feeling beneath the pearly shroud
and a shiver as life continued its journey.

Now she longs for the old embrace
the imprints of sweeter decades.

Too young for a last farewell
she lies a virgin land in the desert.

In Absentia

Waiting for an End

Sitting in the somber corner,
in a library like no other,
forgotten under a layer of lives.

Volumes surrounded him
like the fortress he hoped to erect
years of unending knowledge.

Cripple within the lonely soul
he still dreamed of an encounter
with the true lives of those he sought.

But it was late in the strange alcove,
still as death inside the dark silence
where he pondered every gesture.

It had been decades of abandonment
making worlds to shroud himself in hope
and he wondered how long it would endure.

As if an old monochrome print,
he now appears a mass of wrinkly flesh
dead to the multitudes, he persists.

He may have been a mummy,
star attraction of a musty museum;
perhaps he too was uncertain.

Glaring at the only page he ever knew
he slept with those he so loved;
forgotten as on his first light.

In Absentia

White World

Imagine a day without light,
a sun that dies without warning,
the universe when all stars have perished,
and the waters on Earth reflecting no rainbow.
Picture the deep blue of your eyes,
as it becomes lifeless, white, and dissipates
within the milky way; observe a night thickening,
where the moon is languid in desperation.

Learn to feed a fertile imagination,
walking in a darkness without known end;
around you form the shapes and hues you once knew.
Your heart will be nurtured or it will die.
No need to try and record the world;
memories are all you need; revive your senses
from inside your inner being, infinite as you may be,
the cells remember what once awakened them.

See in the unfathomable obscurity,
dreams never perish, heaven awaits;
your heart larger than the depth yet not traveled,
pleasure immeasurable found within you.
Stars come to be again on the walls inside,
as you invent a universe made for you and me
you close the eyes of a soul where no one may go
to a creation not unlike that which your elegance desired.

So you will see again, fortunate you are,
the creation is yours, you are the mistress
who decides on red, black, or green on this house;
please enter, my secrets to you are revealed.
Night day, day night, white black, light dark,
now all one, now all none, you know it matters not,
a hand on your breast, your heart beats, your chest heaves,
conqueror, in day and night your live forevermore.

In Absentia

Words in Silence

She waved her grace at the passer-by
moving a fragment of her universe
around ripples to echo through space and time.

Her words vanished into unheard waves
as lines in her surroundings traced a story
on the page of a body in full motion.

I wondered why anyone would speak so loudly
when she played a symphony in utter silence
through smiling lips of crimson tenderness.

She danced on a tile floor made of clouds,
sending her message to change all lives,
in a language common through ages and worlds.

Acknowlegements

*These poems have been previously published
in the below listed magazines/journals/periodicals*

"Breaking Away," *Winamop*, March 2019
"Brown Bags," *The Racket Journal*, Vol. 2, # 25, 2020
"Calling in Silence," *Ephemeral Elegies*, March 2020.
"Chest of Riches," *Poetry Pacific*, November 2019.
"Eternity in a Vise," *Wink*, Issue # 3, 2018
"Explorer," *Adelaide*, April 2018
"First Day," *Retreats from Oblivion*, November 2018
"Grace Undercover," *Resonance*, Vol. 3, 2021
"My New Home," *Literary Yard*, September 2020
"Nothing Less," *In Parentheses*, June 2020
"Old Bones in the Forgotten City,"*The Brasilia Review*,
    March 2020
"Opus Mundi," *Datura*, # 3, April 2019
"Silent Walls," *Impspired*, February 2021
"Skeleton Man," *Northwest Indiana Literary Journal*,
    October 2019
"Sleeping Next to her Name," *Rosette Maleficarum*, May 2019
"Thief," *Sandpiper*, Spring 2019
"Tickled in Death," *Sybil*, May 2019
"Touching the Ghost," *Literary Yard*, November 2019
"Under a Golden Blanket," *Erothanatos*, Vol. 13, Issue # 4,
    October 2019
"Unnamed," *Egophobia*, Issue # 57, March 2019
"Virgin Land," *New Reader Magazine*, Vol. 2, Issue # 7, 2019
"White World," *Better than Starbucks*, Vol. 2, Issue # 1,
    January, 2017.
"Words in Silence," *Libretto*, September 2020

Author Profile:

Fabrice Poussin teaches French and English at Shorter University. Author of novels and poetry, his work has appeared in Kestrel, Symposium, La Pensee Universelle, Paris, The Chimes, the Shorter University award winning poetry and arts publication, and many other magazines. His photography has been published in The Front Porch Review, the San Pedro River Review as well as other publications.